Jan. 26. 03
To my darling Brian
To celebrate our Family
with all my Love
Shifra.

MOMENTS

# INTIMACY

LAUGHTER

KINSHIP

© Louise Gubb

# FAMILY

MOMENTS  INTIMACY  LAUGHTER  KINSHIP

HODDER

M·I·L·K

The family is one of nature's masterpieces.

M.I.L.K. began as **a dream**,
became an ambitious adventure,
and gathered strength as it grew.
We see now that it took on **a life of its own**,
ceased to be a project and became instead

# a gift.

The M.I.L.K. Collection is the result of an epic global search for 300 extraordinary and geographically diverse photographs of family life, friendship and love.

This "epic search" took the form of a photographic competition – probably the biggest, and almost certainly the most ambitious of its kind, ever to be conducted. With a world-record prize pool, and renowned photographer Elliott Erwitt as Chief Judge, the M.I.L.K. competition was conceived to attract the work of leading photographers from as many of the world's countries as possible.

We promoted the competition as "the photographic event of our time" and to substantiate this claim set about the exhaustive task of finding and personally inviting photographers to enter from every one of the world's 192 countries.

Our challenge to the photographers was for them to capture and celebrate the essence of humanity, and our judging criteria called for genuine photographic stories conveying real and spontaneous emotion. Ultimately 17,000 photographers from a staggering total of 164 countries participated, among them a myriad of award winners (including at least four Pulitzer Prize winners), professionals and gifted amateurs from six continents. Over 40,000 photographs were submitted – some in lovingly stitched cloth packages, others alongside warm and heartfelt messages of support and encouragement – unforgettable images of human life, from its first fragile moments to its last.

And so the results of this global search are here for you to enjoy. Our hope – that is, the M.I.L.K. team's hope – is that you will look through this *Family* collection and recognize the people in it. Their moments are our moments. The instants of their lives, captured here, are universal.

M.I.L.K. began as a dream, became an ambitious adventure, and gathered strength as it grew. We see now that it took on a life of its own, ceased to be a project, and became instead a gift.

Along with our dreams, we had high ideals for this collection; we demanded absolute excellence and integrity in submission and selection. Tolstoy, in attempting to define "art", wrote that the feelings art evokes must be comprehensible by the mass of people and not just a few. We agree. These images speak to all of us with clarity, universality and – to use that elusive and neglected word – joy.

We salute the men and women who have shaped this project. We hand over ownership of the dream to all who have been involved, because it is no longer ours. Ours was a wisp of an idea, which has been replaced by a tremendous, inspiring reality.

To the brilliant photographers, to Tim Hely Hutchinson who shared my vision for the project at the outset, to Elliott Erwitt, to my friend and M.I.L.K. Project Director Ruth Hamilton, and our skilled colleagues, to my generous family and other friends who kept faith along the way – and to you, as you begin your personal journey through these pages – profound thanks. All these moments of intimacy, laughter and kinship belong to you.

**GEOFF BLACKWELL** M.I.L.K.

JAMES MCBRIDE

The M.I.L.K. Collection is the result of an epic global search for 300 extraordinary and geographically diverse photographs of family life, friendship and love.

In these pages you are holding your own reflection, your own history, frozen and committed to God forever. These photographs reflect a world that will disappear if we allow it. They reflect a world that we are trying to make go away, the way you shoo flies from a room. They also hold evidence of our last and greatest discovery.

We live in a world that is fresh out of discoveries. We have plumbed the planet to its depths. We've walked the ocean floor, blasted into space, built metropolises over what was once forest, discovered the internal combustion engine, created cars, planes, trains and rockets that run on gas, sun rays, algae, popcorn, even soda pop. We've plundered the world's great rivers and seas of fish, algae, microbes, plants, buried treasure, and every living thing. Nearly every spot on the globe has been mapped, chronicled, documented, discussed, mulled over, historicalized, tagged, studied, fictionalized, exploited, polluted, filmed for Hollywood, and manipulated by someone clambering for a buck, yen, marks, pride, their place in history, or some greater glory.

Yet there is no greater miracle than watching a child being born. There is no mightier conquest than to teach a six-year-old the magic of reading. There is no greater force on Earth than the warm breath of a toothless old grandma.

Family is the last and greatest discovery. It is our last miracle.

It's a sad reality that we've entered this new millennium shorn of wisdom, with the same appalling ignorance with which we entered the last: old men still send young men off to die in silly wars; countries are still run by politicians with the kind of ice-cold smiles that keep kids up at night; we still invent numerous ways to gas, annihilate, shoot, maim, kill and destroy each other.

Yet none of those things equals the power of a child's trembling, tapping fingers on a sleeping papa's face. No bomb can destroy the memory of the sweet smell of a mama's breast. No amount of Internet access can replicate the freckle-faced grin of your kid brother who's missing two front teeth.

Family is the last line of reason in a world that still allows 125 million children to go to bed hungry every night. Without it, we are all a tribe of nomads, cut adrift, disconnected, wandering the earth with neither time nor place nor history to give our aching souls a home. We're like strangers at a disco, hundreds of people being lonely together, dancing wildly to some atrocious pounding, then dragging one another to strange quarters to make love at night, only to realize by the dawn's early light that we've made love to a perfect stranger. We all yearn for closeness, yet can't seem to find it in our instant-information-Internet-dot-com age. We've done nothing wrong. It's just that technology has robbed us of miracles. After a lifetime of watching John Wayne take one in the gut for the good guy every Sunday afternoon on the 2:30 movie, we're asked to believe that Jesus Christ died for our sins, that Elijah will return, that Buddha is in all living things, and that Allah is God, and it's wearing on us. We're being globalized to death, our souls and history plagiarized by anxious souls angling for a share of the percentage, while our families and tribes and cultures slowly and quietly vanish.

Someone once said that if we wanted to end all wars we should issue credit cards to our enemies. Let them buy jeans and tennis shoes and t-shirts with poster-sized ads for Tommy Hilfiger. I don't agree. I say let the grandmas of the planet stand atop the world and have the soapbox equivalent of a jazz solo. Give the grandmothers of this world eight bars and there would be no blues. Because grandmas from the Iraqi nation to the Iroquois nation, from Australia to the Andes, they would not have it. They would not hear of it.

The images in this book are about all the rough, tough, laughing, scraggly, diaper-pooping, kick-ass grandchildren of every one of those grandmas. They reach beyond the atrocity of mindless developers and nameless corporations who sandbag our world, building faceless modular homes and bulldozing trails and forests that once held dirt, sweat, toil, wildlife and children's footprints. They chronicle what lasts and will always last: a mother's love, a grandpa's pride, a child's giggle, a father's sorrow. Family love is stronger than steel and concrete. Family love is like the wind: instinctive, raw, fragile, beautiful, at times angry, but always unstoppable. It is our collective breath. It is the world's greatest force.

Close your eyes and listen. What do you hear? The beating sound you hear is not your heart. It is the sound of a thousand sewing needles. The world is no melting pot, but rather a giant quilt made up of millions of tiny patches, all of which create a beautiful mosaic that covers and warms us all. For that reason, this book is not merely a group of majestic photographs, but rather a family album, and these are our relatives. Each of us has had the old Greek uncle who paces the balcony of his disheveled apartment, hands clasped behind his back, cigarette between his fingers, ruminating with abandon about the government, the price of eggs, his friend the plumber, the war, the Lottery, the cost of shoes, the good old days. Every one of us has had the two aunts who haven't spoken to each other in fifty years; who hasn't had the wacky cousin that nearly poked his eye with a fork, or the sister who ate the cornflake sandwich? What is funnier than two Islamic brothers yelling at each other over the cost of a brake job? Or two Jewish grandmothers quibbling over a groom and saying, "Let's check his teeth." You haven't lived till you've dangled spit from a four-storey window with your kid sister or, better yet, let her dangle you out the first floor window by the heels. What is more American – Danish – Italian – your choice – than the yelling, screaming, crying, quibbling, swiping and bartering of food and candy of French siblings … no, Algerian siblings … no, Nigerian siblings … all of the above?

It is the absurdity of family life, the raggedness of it, that is at once its redemption and its true nobility. It is that raggedness that binds us, and we must not allow it to slip away. Life's not a perfect thing. It is a raggedy, funky experience, full of awful timing, sisters who tattletale, brothers who tease, horrid songs by distant old relatives, daddies with bad breath, moms who eat leftovers, smelly old grandpas led to the bathroom by reluctant young charges, alcoholic aunts, cigarette-fouled rooms, pissed-off wives, boys with pockets full of string, laughing cousins, papas who pass away, old people who die slowly, and dogs who poop on the living room floor.

The world needs more of this kind of funk, not less. We need more ancient Land Rovers packed with desert tribesmen families; and school buses, full of tired African fathers en route to work, with goats tied to the roof; we need grandma's hands; grandpa's urinal; mother's toothbrush; Tateh's easy laughter; Uncle Ahmed's ancient shaving gear; and our great-aunt Lisa from Ireland who likes to eat dinner without her wig or her false teeth. We need more old Chevys full of three generations of Cubans, and vans loaded with Turks trekking across Europe – Gypsies, gentiles, freaks, fat tourists all. Because without these people, we have no funk, and without funk, what are we? Greaseless, clean, lifeless blobs, living the equivalent of fast food, wearing the same clothes, driving the same cars, living the same clone-like existences, indifferent to the very things that make us special: our families. Our tribes. All of which make us one.

Tribalism is not a bad word. It does not mean war. It does not mean separation. It does not mean mine is better than yours. It means listening to our collective invisible drum. Close your eyes and put your hand to your heart and beyond the sound of a thousand sewing needles, you will hear the sound of hearts beating all across the world. They are the same heart. They are a collective heart. We. Ours. Not they nor them. It is the heart of a family. It is our song. Yet we are not listening. Only when the sound ceases, do we ache to hear it. Tamás Kovác's photo on page 107 of the howling relatives standing over the beautiful boy in his coffin, his lifeless gaze making you wish with all your heart that he'd wake up laughing and saying, "Papa! Papa! I was only playing!" Knowing he will not. Ever. Only when our heart breaks do we listen for it. Only when death is about do we ache to hear our most sacred and beautiful song, the sound of our collective heartbeat. But then it is too late.

I believe that every person who has died – in slavery, in war, in the holocaust, in death camps, in terrorist attacks, through man-made destruction and God-made plague, drought and starvation – has died so that the rest of us can live. I believe that every howling, graveyard cry that every mother has ever hollered to heaven has been a scream to the gods to have mercy on the rest of us, so that each of us in our own families might live better and with more mercy. So sweet and precious is family life, so merciful it is. And so horrible it is when it is taken away by someone other than God. We are not qualified to kill our own. We are only human beings. We are only a family. We are not qualified to kill our family. That has to come from outside us. That has to come from beyond.

In the images that follow, you will witness not just the extraordinary work of great men and women, but the humble offerings of artists who recognize that we are but a pinprick in history, that God can fit infinity on the head of a pin or stretch a moment into an everlasting infinity. Photographers wander the earth like nomads, thousands of them, foot soldiers of our imagination, writing stories with light, shutter speed, content and images. They are our combat units for artistic expression, each capturing their own truth: paparazzi, artists, journalists, fashion and wedding photographers, all; they are soothsayers, bent on capturing the tricksters and shapeshifters known as human emotion.

There's a reason why photographer Anne Bayin of Toronto, Canada, woke up one morning a few years ago, hauled all of her lenses, gear, cameras, and filters onto an airplane, flew to New York City at her own expense, and shot pictures of the annual Easter Parade. Then one day her trained gaze fell upon a dowdy plaster wall in an apartment just blocks from her house, and she saw another part of America's checkered past, the singed earth of Vietnam. She placed Kim Phuc, who was scorched by an American napalm attack in her village in 1972 and whose horrible childhood image was burned into the collective memory of the world, in front of the dowdy plaster wall holding her beautiful one-year-old son, and we have redemption. We have hope. We have the promise that from the greatest sufferings come the brightest tomorrows. That miracle is borne out of the love within us.

Many years ago, a young American mother named Agnes Frakes pointed out images all around her tiny Nebraska town to her four-year-old son Bill: a cat's shadow, a pool of oil beneath a car, his own name etched in a cookie tray of caramel popcorn. The boy looked at the objects and saw nothing. "Look again," she said. "There is always more there than what your eye sees..." Twenty-five years later the boy became one of the most accomplished sports photographers in the world. He stood on a bridge in Miami Beach and captured the carefree couple pedalling a tandem bicycle on pages 88–89 – in one shot. "I can see at speeds that no one else can see," Bill says. "Most good photographers can." A Jewish photographer from Brooklyn named Hazel Hankin wandered Mexico seeking God's light and caught it in the majestic face of the grandmother on page 130 – in a Catholic church, no less. A young South African soldier named Adriaan Oosthuizen returned home from a desperate civil war in Namibia to an indifferent South Africa and found himself banished, with his hippie long hair and Scottish skirts, to the Geocap Nature Reserve, more than 550 kilometres from Cape Town, where a cheap single lens reflex camera gave him freedom to explore his favorite aspect – color – color that was free of the chains of apartheid that were his country's tragic legacy. His image of a beautiful old soldier and his companion, taken in London, graces pages 100–101.

These men and women often cannot explain, even to themselves, why they walk the earth with a box that holds a piece of glass called a lens which yields invisible power. A camera lens is pure as air, clean of prejudice, free of the dirt and mental baggage that cloud our vision, and when these artists apply their visual switches to this simple object, we see magic. Photographers are a bit like jazz musicians.

**JAMES MCBRIDE** SOUTH NYACK, NY

Innocence is the child, and forgetfulness, a new beginning,
a game, a self-rolling wheel, a first movement,
a Holy Yea.

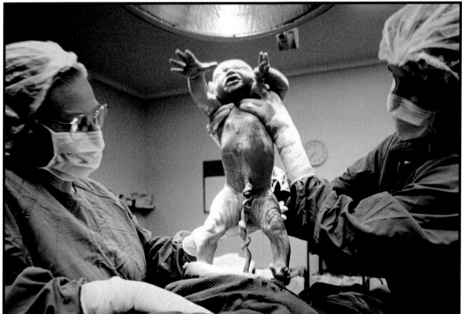

© Tony McDonough

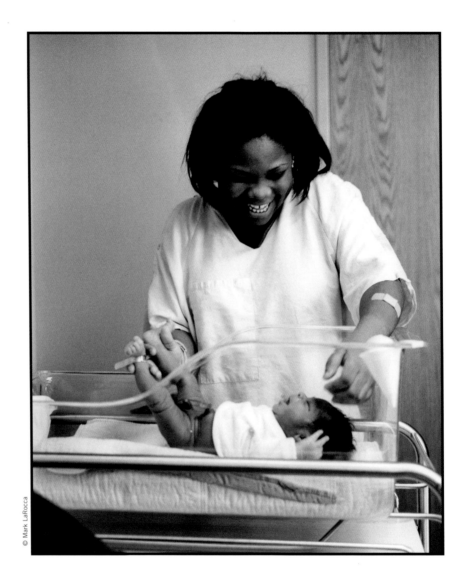

© Mark LaRocca

I am the stem that fed the fruit, the link that joins you to the night.

[JUDITH WRIGHT]

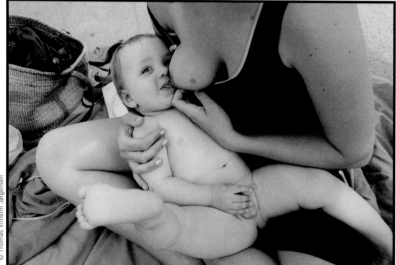

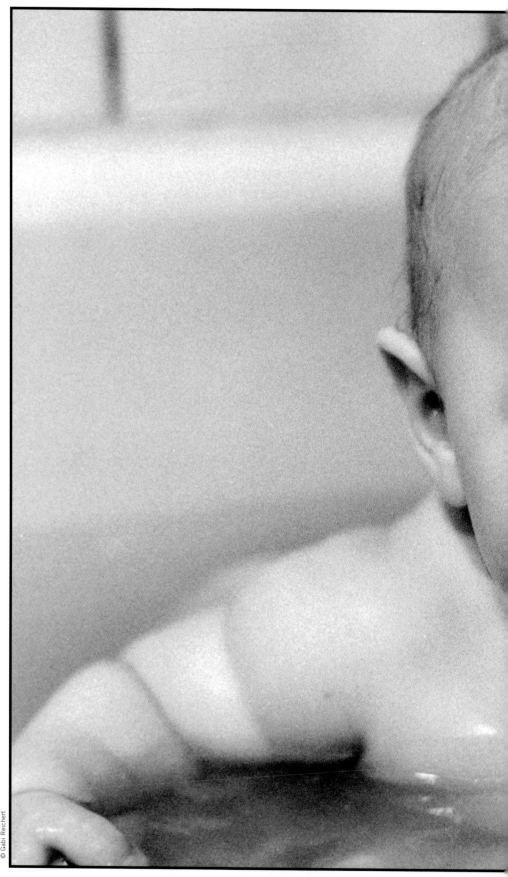

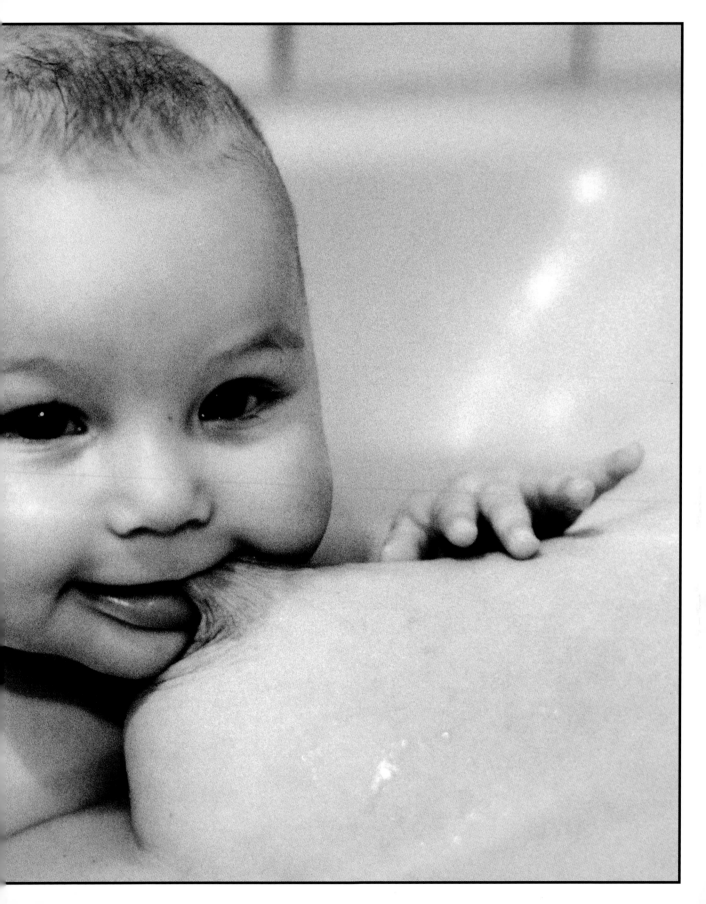

We find a delight in the beauty and happiness of children that makes the heart too big for the body.

© Christel Dhuit

One must ask children and birds how cherries and strawberries taste.

[GOETHE]

Life delights in life.

[WILLIAM BLAKE]

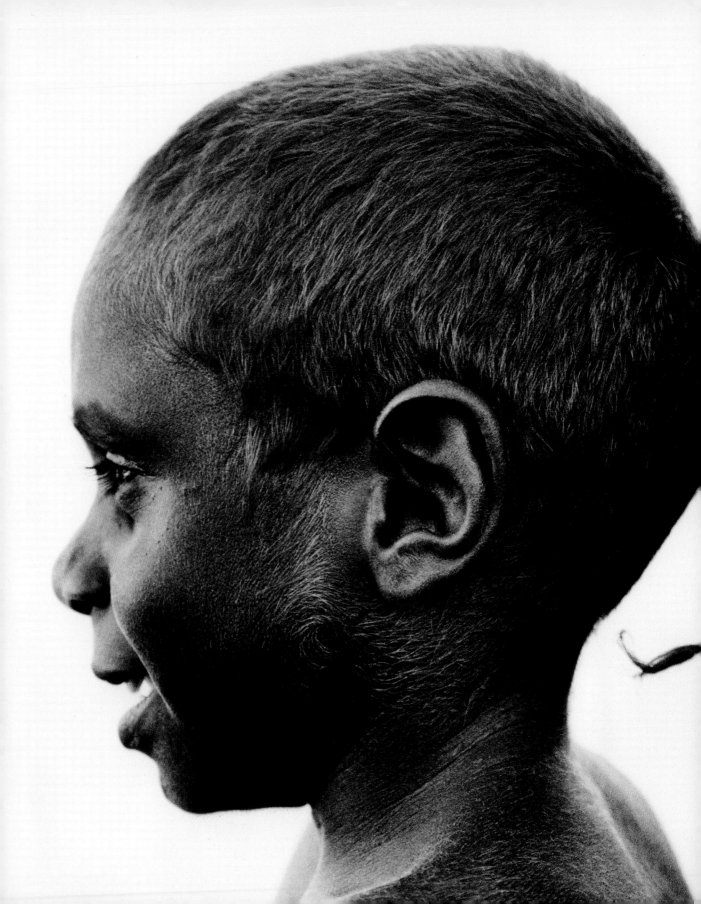

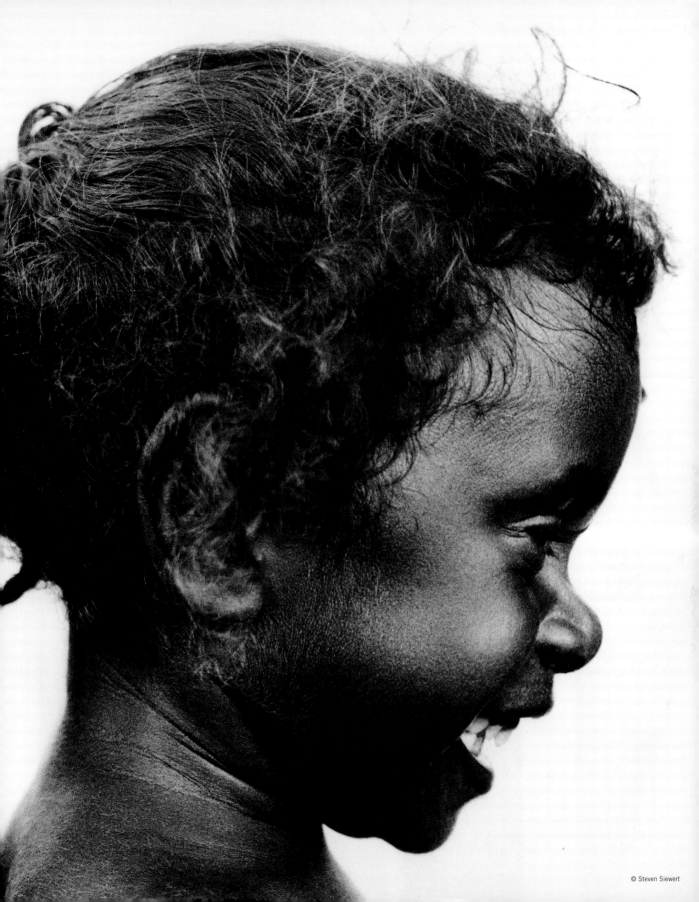

Thee lift me, and I'll lift thee,

and we'll ascend together.

[QUAKER PROVERB]

© Philip Kuruvita

To have joy one must share it. Happiness was born a $twin$.

[LORD BYRON]

Children's faces looking up, holding

wonder

like a cup.

[SARA TEASDALE]

© Michael Agelopas

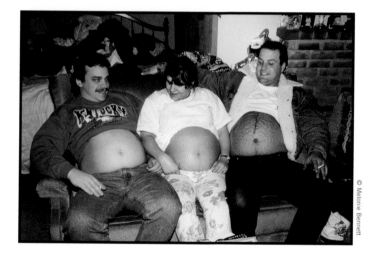

© Melonie Bennett

It is the absurdity of family life, the raggedness of it,
that is at once its redemption and its true nobility.

[JAMES MCBRIDE]

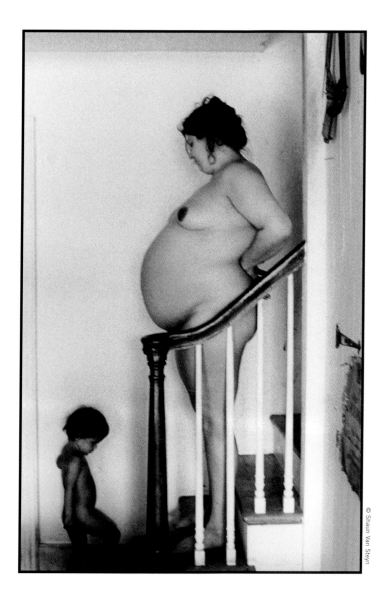

© Shaun Van Steyn

Oh what a power is **motherhood**.

[EURIPIDES]

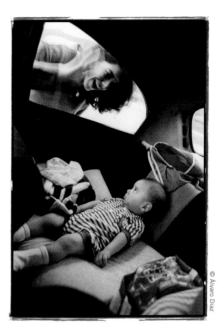

You may give them your love,
but not your thoughts,
for they have their own thoughts.
You may house their bodies,

## but not their souls,

for their souls dwell in the house of tomorrow,
which you cannot visit,
even in your dreams.

[KAHLIL GIBRAN]

So many scars, my arms, my back.
I thought I would never marry, no-one would love me.
But I was so wrong. This picture of me, and my Thomas, my angel —

# it's a picture of love.

[KIM PHUC]

© Guan Cheong Wong

Hold tenderly that which you cherish.

[BOB ALBERTI]

© Tong Wang

© Victor Englebert

It is not flesh and blood,

but the heart which makes us fathers and sons.

[FRIEDRICH VON SCHILLER]

When a child is born, a father is born.

[FREDERICK BUECHNER]

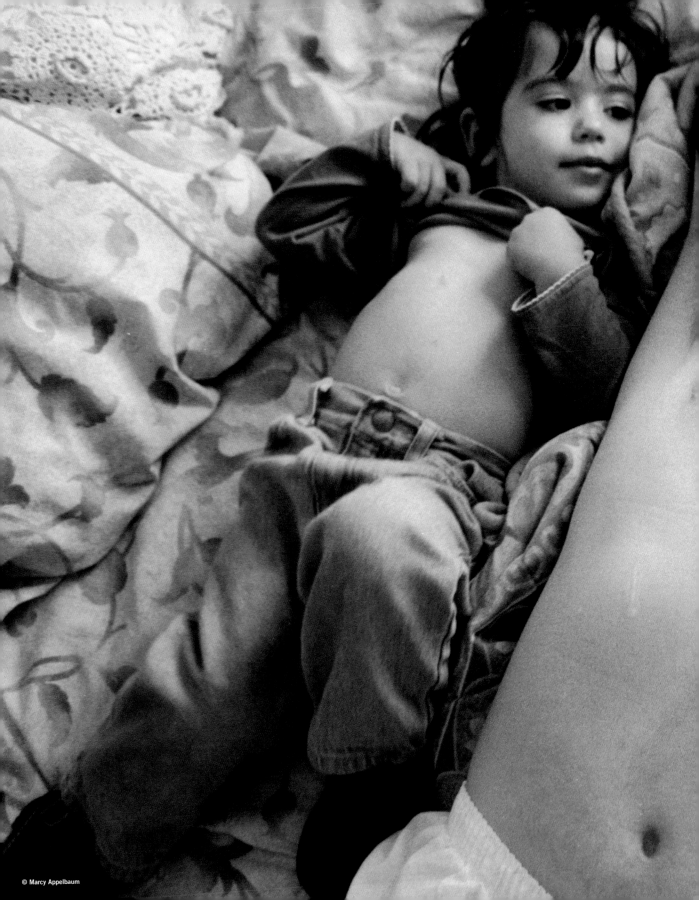

The family – that dear octopus
from whose tentacles
we never quite escape,
nor in our innermost hearts quite wish to.

[DOROTHY GLADYS SMITH]

© Georgina Lucock

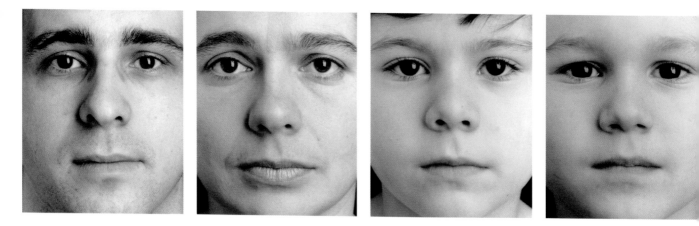

Close your eyes and put your hand to your heart, you will hear the sounds...

© Petra Stepan

of hearts beating all across the world. They are the *same heart*.

[JAMES MCBRIDE]

You cannot catch a child's spirit by running after it.

You must stand still and for love it will soon itself return.

[ARTHUR MILLER]

Joy is not in things, it is in us.

[RICHARD WAGNER]

# know me true.

I live for those who love me, for those who

[GEORGE LINNAEUS BANKS]

© Les Slesnick

Each family, however modest its origin, possesses its own particular tale of the past —
a tale which can bewitch us with as great a sense of **insistent romance**
as can ever the tradition of kings.

[LLEWELLYN POWYS]

Other things may change us, but we start and end with family.

[ANTHONY BRANDT]

Without a family, man, alone in the world,

trembles with the cold.

[ANDRE MAUROIS]

I want to stimulate in people a greater awareness of our common humanity by looking into that most human experience – dying and death. I do so in the hope that this will evoke more compassion for oneself and for others.

[MORRIE SCHWARTZ]

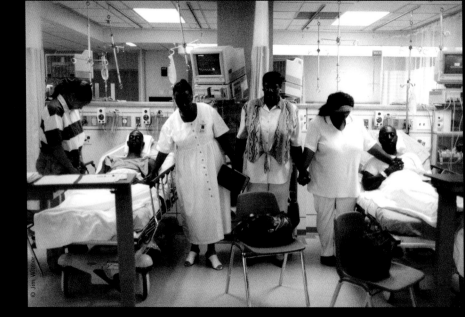

...love, the only survival,
the only meaning.

[THORNTON WILDER]

So sweet and precious is family life…

[JAMES MCBRIDE]

Where there is love, there is life.

[MAHATMA GANDHI]

A happy marriage is a long conversation which always seems too short.

Love does not consist in gazing at each other...

but in looking outward together in the same direction.

[ANTOINE SAINT-EXUPERY]

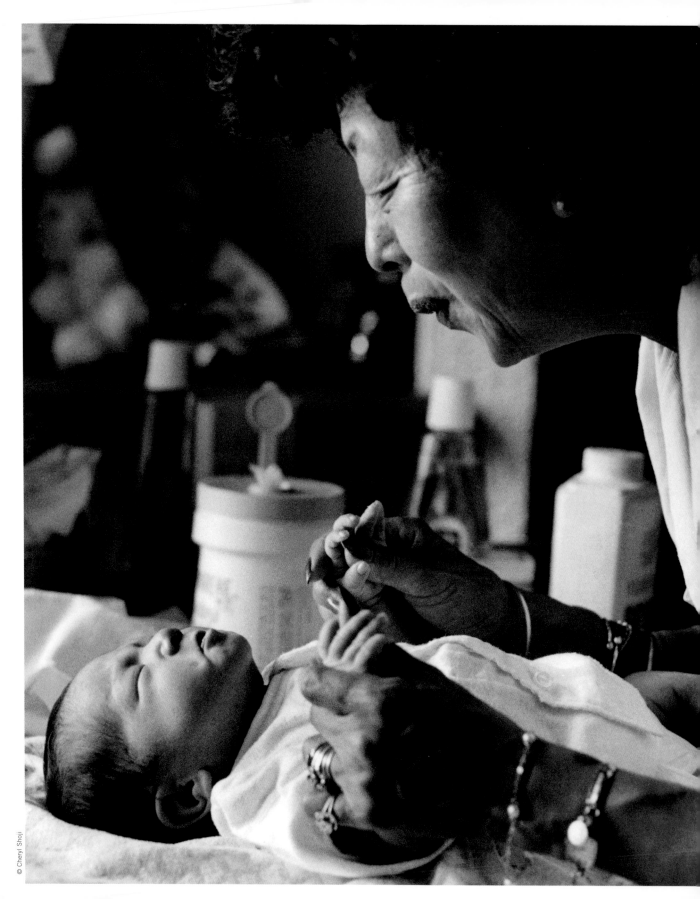

The world will never starve for want of wonders,

but only for want of **wonder**.

[G K CHESTERTON]

Wisdom begins in wonder.

[SOCRATES]

Seek the wisdom of the ages,

© Peter Thomann

…but look at the world through the eyes of a child.

[RON WILD]

© Guus Rijven

© David Williams

Family faces are *magic* mirrors.

[GAIL LUMET BUCKLEY]

Family is the last and greatest discovery…
It is our last miracle.

[JAMES MCBRIDE]

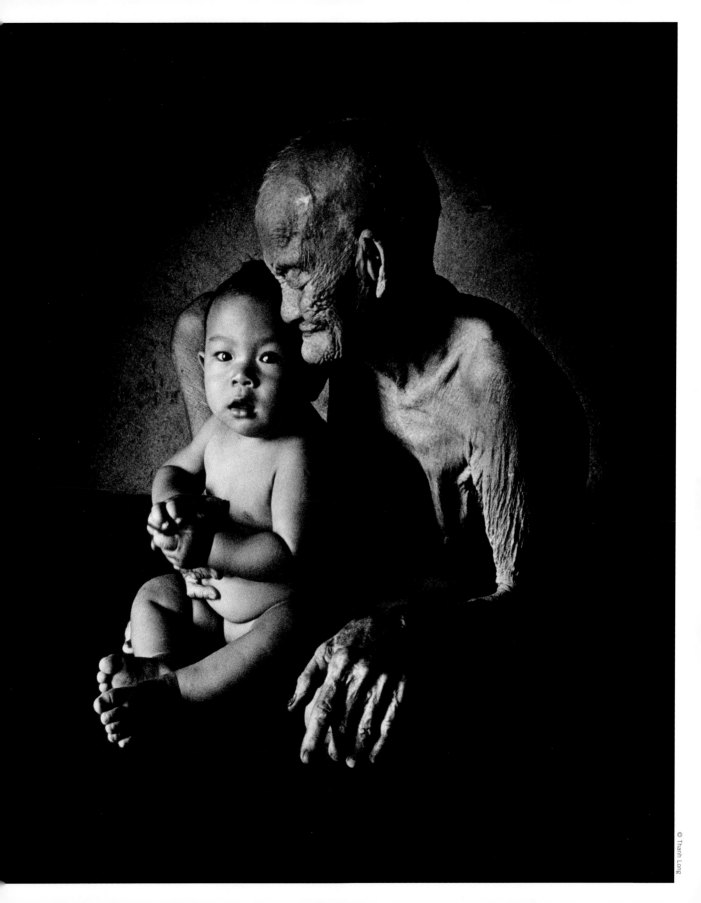

Photographers wander the earth like nomads,

thousands of them,

foot soldiers of our imagination,

writing stories with light, shutter speed, content and images.

### Michael Agelopas
USA

Michael Agelopas was born in Maryland, USA, and was introduced to photography by his father. He has been a professional photographer for over 20 years.

© 1988 Michael Agelopas

On the island of Chios in Greece, five sisters share a village bench. By chance or by habit, they sit in chronological order.

Nikon F3, 135 mm, Kodak Kodachrome/135, Exp. f8-1/60

### Kris Allan
UK

Kris Allan is a self-taught photographer who started his photographic career by documenting life at Wandsworth Prison, London. Since then, Kris's images have been exhibited in a variety of locations, including the ICA in London and the Dutch Institute of Photography in Rotterdam.

© 1997 Kris Allan

Father and son captured at the Goldstone soccer ground in Hove, England.

Olympus OM1N, 50 mm, Kodak Tri-X 400/135, Exp. N/A

### Marcy Appelbaum
USA

Marcy Appelbaum received a photography degree with honors from the Southeast Center for Photographic Studies in Daytona, Florida. She worked as a staff photographer on a variety of newspapers until 1993 when she started her freelance career. Marcy is a winning photographer in the *Communication Arts* juried competition.

© 1998 Marcy Appelbaum

In Jacksonville, Florida, USA, two-year-old Rachel is curious to see if her belly button matches her father's.

Nikon N90, 35 mm, Kodak Tri-X/135, Exp. f2-1/30

### Stefano Azario
UK

Stefano Azario is a photographer internationally known for his work with children. His images have appeared on the covers of *Vogue Bambini*, as well as in advertising campaigns for Gap Kids and Baby Gap. Stefano also works in reportage photography, including assignments for Condé Nast *Traveller* magazine.

© 1999 Stefano Azario

Like mother, like daughter – at a New York airport, there's still time for nine-month-old Verity and her mother Lydzia to play before the long flight home to England.

Konika Hexar, 35 mm, Kodak Tri-X/135, Exp. N/A

### Steven Baldwin
USA

Steven Baldwin is a semi-professional photographer. Originally based in New York, he now works from San Francisco.

© 1981 Steven Baldwin

Standing ovation – a man's rendition of a popular song is well received by his family at a street dinner in the village of Pisoniano, near Rome, in Italy.

Leica M4-P, 35 mm, Kodachrome 64/135, Exp. f4-1/2

### Juan P Barragán
ECUADOR

Born in Ecuador, Juan P Barragán studied physics in Boston, USA, and psychology in Geneva, Switzerland. Currently he operates his own company, Acción Creativa, and is Chief Editor at *Sin Limites*, a prestigious youth magazine in Ecuador.

© 1998 Juan P Barragán

Keeping tradition alive near Lake San Pablo, Ecuador. Four generations of an Imbabura Indian family prepare their hair in the time-honoured way – from right to left: Mama-Rosa, Rosa, Rosa Elena and Miriam.

Nikon F2, 180 mm, Ilford/135, Exp. N/A

### Anne Bayin
CANADA

Anne Bayin is a Toronto-based television producer and writer. Her production credits include the CBS flagship current affairs programme *The Journal*. She has studied with the renowned photographers Freeman Patterson and Len Jenshel. Anne has travelled extensively with her photography and has had several exhibitions.

© Nick Ut, AP/AAP

Kim Phuc was the subject of the most famous picture of the Vietnam War. Taken in 1972, the photograph showed Kim – "the girl in the picture" – badly burned by napalm.

© 1995 Anne Bayin

Kim grew up thinking boys would find her unattractive because of her scars, but today she is married and living in Canada. She is a Goodwill Ambassador for UNESCO. This photograph celebrates the first birthday of Kim's son, Thomas.

Nikon F601, 35–70 mm, Kodak Gold 200/135, Exp. N/A

### Melonie Bennett
USA

Melonie Bennett grew up on a farm in Maine, USA, where she became interested in photography. She studied the subject at college and now displays her images at local colleges and galleries, and at national exhibitions.

© 1997 Melonie Bennett

Family likeness – brothers-in-law Jim and Scott compare themselves to nine-months' pregnant Mary, at home in Gorham, Maine, USA.

Pentax K1000, 35 mm, Kodak Tri-X/135, Exp. f11-1/60

### Gunars Binde
LATVIA

Gunars Binde is a highly respected photographer who began his association with photography in 1958. In 1970, he was chosen as one of the top 10 photographers in Europe. He has participated in numerous exhibitions and has won many photographic awards. Gunars was made a Master of Art Emeritus in Lithuania and has the honorary title HKT in Austria. Today he lives in Riga, Latvia.

© Gunars Binde [date N/A]

The family problem – views are aired on a park bench in Moscow, Russia.

Saliut TAIR 3, 5.6/300 mm, Foto/180, Exp. 1/60

### Shauna Angel Blue
USA

Shauna Angel Blue is a mother of two, a grandmother of three, and a keen amateur photographer. Recently she graduated from Columbia College in Chicago, with a Master of Fine Arts in photography.

© 1997 Shauna Angel Blue

Chicago, Illinois, USA – dressed in her favourite tutu, two-year-old Rose dances to the tune of her mother's harp.

Nikon, 50 mm, Kodak Tri-X/135, Exp. f11-1/500

### Gerald Botha
SOUTH AFRICA

Gerald Botha was born in Cape Town and now lives in Durban, South Africa. He has worked as a professional photographer for the last 10 years, concentrating on studio, fashion, wedding and architectural photography.

© 1997 Gerald Botha

Good morning in Durban, South Africa – the photographer's wife Aileen greets their three-month-old son Eden.

Canon EOS 5, 135 mm, Fuji/135, Exp. f5.6-1/60

### Paul Carter
USA

Paul Carter is a self-taught photographer. He graduated in journalism in 1972 from the University of Maryland, followed by military service with the US Navy Submarine Service. In a varied journalistic career spanning 25 years, Paul has worked as a reporter, editor, photographer or photo-editor with seven different newspapers.

© 1993 Paul Carter

A gentle smile from mother to son in Eugene, Oregon, USA. Nano, 85, suffers from arthritis but is cared for at home by her son, Doug. After an afternoon reading to his mother, Doug lifts her carefully back to bed.

Leica M6, 35 mm, Kodak Tri-X/135, Exp. N/A

### Roberto Colacioppo
ITALY

Roberto Colacioppo is a professional photographer based in Lanciano, Italy. He specializes in wedding, portrait and fashion photography.

© 1999 Roberto Colacioppo

A great-grandmother's heartfelt embrace of a young bride. The old lady, 97, and her great-granddaughter are the only family members who still live in the mountain village of Roccaspinalveti, Italy.

Nikon F4S, 2.8/80–200 mm, Kodak/135, Exp. N/A

### Eddee Daniel
USA

Eddee Daniel has been a photographer and a teacher for over 20 years. He is based in the USA and works in a range of styles, from documentary to experimental. Eddee is also a writer and has combined photography with poetry in a number of his exhibits.

© 1987 Eddee Daniel

A moment of discovery in Sauk City, Wisconsin, USA, as one-year-old Chelsea realizes where the music is coming from.

Nikon FE, 50 mm, Kodak Tri-X/135, Exp. N/A

### Rajib De
INDIA

Rajib De was born in Chandannagore, India. After graduating in 1987, he joined the staff of a leading newspaper, the *Telegraph*. For the last five years, he has been senior staff photographer at the *Statesman* in Calcutta. In 1995 Rajib won the first of three awards from UNESCO. He has also won two awards from the Photographic Association of India.

© 1994 Rajib De

Three-year-old Tito follows in the footsteps of an 82-year-old professor on an afternoon stroll through Calcutta, India.

Nikon F3, 2.8/135 mm, Orow/135, Exp. f4-1/125

### Christel Dhuit
NEW ZEALAND

Christel Dhuit was born and educated in France before moving to London. She is now based in New Zealand and is completing a graphic design and photography degree in Auckland. She is also involved in freelance photographic work.

© 1999 Christel Dhuit

They may be twins, but their reactions are very different. Five-month-old sisters in Auckland, New Zealand.

Canon A1, 50 mm, Kodak T-max 400/135, Exp. N/A

### Álvaro Diaz
BRAZIL

Álvaro Diaz began taking photographs in 1979, and now teaches photography at the State University of Santa Caterina in South Brazil. Currently he is involved in a Federal Government project to create a museum of twentieth-century photographs for use by high school students.

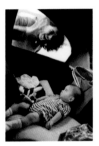

© 1998 Álvaro Diaz

10-month-old Gabriel and his mother, Paula. The photographer captured this picture of his son in Florianopolis, Brazil.

Nikon FM2, 24 mm, Kodak Plus-X/135, Exp. f2.8-1/4

### Lyn Dowling
AUSTRALIA

Lyn Dowling is a trained pharmacist in Brisbane, Australia. She began part-time study of photography in 1994 and it has been her serious interest ever since.

© 1994 Lyn Dowling

"Ma" and me – Rebecca, aged 20 months, and her grandmother "Ma" share the simple pleasures of a street festival in Brisbane, Australia.

Olympus OM1, 50 mm, Agfa APX/135, Exp. N/A

### Victor Englebert
USA

Victor Englebert is a self-taught photographer, a writer and a publisher of 10 photography books. To date, he has lived among 30 different tribes across three continents, and his resulting photo stories have appeared in numerous publications including *National Geographic*, *Paris Match*, *International Wildlife* and the London *Sunday Times*.

© 1981 Victor Englebert

In the Amazon rainforest of Brazil, a Yanomami Indian relaxes in a hammock made of bark strips and plays with his young grandson.

Leica M2, 35 mm, Kodachrome 64/135, Exp. f2.8-1/30

### Paz Errázuriz
CHILE

Paz Errázuriz is a self-taught photographer from Santiago, Chile. She studied education at the Catholic University in Santiago and, after graduation, worked as a primary school teacher. After leaving the teaching profession, she became an independent photographer for magazines and Fundacion Andes. She was awarded a Guggenheim Fellowship in 1987, and has had two books published.

© 1994 Paz Errázuriz

Waiting patiently – in a remote fishing village in southern Chile, bar owners Mr and Mrs Andrade ponder when their next customer will arrive.

Nikon F3, 35 mm, Kodak Tri-X/135, Exp. f4-1/30

### James Fassinger
USA

James Fassinger gained most of his early photographic experience through internships at newspapers in America. He then travelled to Prague, in the Czech Republic, and became photo editor for the country's first English language newspaper, *Prognosis*. Currently he lives in Prague and works freelance throughout Europe.

© 1998 James Fassinger

Mirror image – identical twins take a springtime stroll along the banks of the Vltava River in Prague, Czech Republic.

Nikon F3 HP, 55 mm, Kodak T-max 400/135, Exp. f5.6-1/500

### Raymond Field
SOUTH AFRICA

Raymond Field is a self-taught photographer. Currently he works for an engineering and mining publication based in Johannesburg, South Africa.

© 1992 Raymond Field

The rhythm of the beat sets toddlers dancing to the delight of onlookers in Johannesburg, South Africa.

Minolta 500, 35–70 mm, Ilford HP5/135, Exp. f5.6-1/125

### Katherine Fletcher
USA

Katherine Fletcher holds a Bachelor of Fine Arts degree in photography. She runs her own business, Unforgettable Images, in Omaha, Nebraska, specializing in journalistic wedding photography.

© 1997 Katherine Fletcher

At a wedding in Omaha, Nebraska, USA, a young guest hides her eyes as a newly married couple share a kiss; her young friend is unperturbed.

Canon A2, 28–70 mm, Kodak/135, Exp. f5.6-1/90

### Bill Frakes
USA

Bill Frakes is an eminent professional photographer who has worked in over 50 countries and is currently contracted to *Sports Illustrated*. His photographs have appeared for the past 20 years in leading magazines and newspapers, and his advertising clients have included Nikon, Kodak and IBM. Bill is a Pulitzer Prize winner and a former Newspaper Photographer of the Year.

© Bill Frakes [date N/A]

In tandem – a novel way of moving house captured on film in Miami Beach, Florida, USA.

N/A

### Tomas D W Friedmann
ITALY

Tomas D W Friedmann, the son of a photographer mother, arrived in New York from Israel in 1951. Here he won an award in a "young photographers" competition run by *Life* magazine, but could not find work as a photographer. Instead Tomas started his own agency – Pip Photos Inc. – which was so successful that he retired to the Italian Riviera in 1970. Four agents in New York, Tokyo, Germany and Switzerland market his images today.

© 1962 Tomas D W Friedmann

Protected and loved – in the Masailand of Tanzania, a Masai mother gently carries her young child.

Nikon, Nikormat 35–75 mm, Kodachrome/135, Exp. f8-1/250

### Louise Gubb
SOUTH AFRICA

Louise Gubb has been a freelance photojournalist for over 20 years. She has worked extensively in Africa, and has lived and worked in the USA and the Middle East. Currently Louise works for SABA Press, and resides in Cape Town, South Africa.

© 1999 Louise Gubb

The simple love of a family bonds a father and son beside the Fiherenana River in Madagascar. The Malagasy people come to this area to mine for sapphires.

Nikon F90, 35 mm, Kodak E100 SW/135, Exp. f5.6-1/125

### Hazel Hankin
USA

Hazel Hankin teaches photography at the City College of New York and works as a freelance photographer. Her photographs have appeared in *Double Take* magazine, Graphis Press international journalism books and Life's *Album of the Year* 1996. Her work is also represented in the permanent collection of the Brooklyn Museum of Art, the Houston Museum of Fine Arts, and the MAK Center for Art and Architecture in Los Angeles.

© 1996 Hazel Hankin

Face of ages – the experiences of a lifetime are etched on the face of a Mexican matriarch. As she sits serenely in the church in Michoacán, Mexico, a child nestles in close.

Canon F1, 100 mm, Kodak T-max 3200/135, Exp. N/A

### Joan Harrison
USA

Joan Harrison is Professor of Art at Long Island University in Brookville, New York. She works as an "art maker", using techniques including photography, collage and digital imaging.

© 1988 Joan Harrison

A portrait of family life as parents Lynne and John relax with "Little John" at their home in Martha's Vineyard, Massachusetts, USA.

Olympus OM2, 35 mm, Kodak Tri-X/135, Exp. N/A

### Stephen Hathaway
UK

Stephen Hathaway has a Masters degree in corporate design/graphics. After working in graphic design, followed by a period in advertising, Stephen decided to move into photography full time. He has worked on advertising accounts as well as pursuing personal projects, and has had two recent exhibitions in London.

© 1999 Stephen Hathaway

Charles and his grandson Richard are deep in conversation as they sit in Soho Square, London, England.

Canon EOS 1NH, 70–210 mm, Kodak Tri-X/135, Exp. f5.6-1/250

### Steve Hotson
UK

Steve Hotson was born in Nottingham, England. He travelled widely around the world before studying design and photography at South Nottingham College. Today Steve is a freelancer specializing in documentary, reportage and wedding photography.

© 1996 Steve Hotson

Sisters Dorothy and Annie, both over 90, enjoy a quiet moment together. They have taken a seat opposite a country church to watch a wedding party in Owthorpe, in Nottinghamshire, England.

Nikon FM2, 50 mm, Ilford XP2/135, Exp. f5.6-1/250

### Andrei Jewell
NEW ZEALAND

Andrei Jewell was born in Zimbabwe and is now based in New Zealand. He is a self-taught photographer and has been involved in the industry for over 15 years. He is an associate member of the New Zealand Professional Photographers Association and a winner of their Gold Award.

© 1989 Andrei Jewell

The beautiful mountain scenery of Zanskar in the Indian Himalayas is the setting for a twilight stroll. In a region which is snow-covered for most of the year, Norbu and his young granddaughter make the most of the warm sunshine.

Nikon F3, 135 mm, Kodachrome/135, Exp. f3.5-1/125

### Thomas Vilhelm Jørgensen
SPAIN

Thomas Vilhelm Jørgensen was born in Denmark and graduated in communications from Roskilde University Centre in 1994. He became a freelance photographer after postgraduate study at the London College of Printing, and now works from Barcelona in Spain.

© 1998 Thomas Vilhelm Jørgensen

Benjamin, almost one year old, with his mother, Rigmor. Mother and son were photographed while on holiday in Gava near Barcelona, Spain.

Nikon F3, 28 mm, Kodak Tri-X/135, Exp. N/A

### Jenny Jozwiak
USA

Jenny Jozwiak studied photography at City College in New York. Since graduating, she has worked in portraiture, photojournalism, fashion and travel photography. Her personal work has been exhibited in various galleries throughout New York and in several private collections, and she has produced slide presentations of her images for the Museum of Natural History, Time-Life Building and Columbia University.

© 1997 Jenny Jozwiak

Holding the baby – by the Kali Ghandaki River in Nepal, a young girl cares for her brother while her parents work in the fields. The children's grandmother spins cotton-wool in the doorway.

Nikon F3, 50 mm, Velvia/135, Exp. f11-1/125

### Kelvin Patrick Jubb
AUSTRALIA

Kelvin Jubb is a shipping clerk who lives in Sydney, Australia. He studied art and graphic design at high school and then photography at community college. Previously he specialized in landscapes, but the arrival of his own son sparked an interest in capturing the spirit of new life.

© 1999 Kelvin Patrick Jubb

Fewer than 24 hours have elapsed since this baby was born. In a busy hospital ward in Penrith, Australia, the baby is cradled by his mother as he experiences his first bath.

Pentax SF7, Macro 0.188–1 m, Ilford XP2 Super/135, Exp. N/A

### Abu Taher Khokon
BANGLADESH

Abu Taher Khokon has been a photographer in Bangladesh for over 15 years, having graduated with a BEGART Diploma in Photography in Dhaka. He won the Accu Award in Japan in 1993, 1994 and 1996, followed by the UN Award and the AFEJ Award of Sri Lanka in 1998.

© 1999 Abu Taher Khokon

Afternoon sleep in Khulna, Bangladesh – while a family takes a rest in the hot sultry summer, only the mother stays awake.

Nikon FM2, 24–50 mm, Fuji/135, Exp. f5.6-1/60

### John Kaplan
USA

John Kaplan is an associate professor at the University of Florida where he teaches photography and design. He was awarded the Pulitzer Prize for Feature Photography in 1992. Earlier, in 1989, John received the Robert F Kennedy Award for outstanding work in photographing the disadvantaged in the United States. In the same year, he was named National Newspaper Photographer of the Year in the Picture of the Year Award.

© 1988 John Kaplan

A grandmother's love – clothed in animal skins, a nomadic peasant cuddles her grandchild in the remote Namtso region of Tibet.

Nikon F5, 300 mm, Fuji/135, Exp. f4-1/1000

© 1998 John Kaplan

Double happiness – as Xia Yongqing, 84, and his nephew Yang Ziyun, 82, share a joke in the village of Nanyang in the Sichuan province of China.

Nikon F5, 35 mm, Fuji/135, Exp. f4-1/250

### Thomas Patrick Kiernan
IRELAND

Thomas Patrick Kiernan was born in Ireland and developed an interest in photography after seeing Cartier-Bresson and Kertesz exhibitions in New York. In between summer jobs, Thomas pursues his passion for photography by working in India and Egypt.

© 1994 Thomas Patrick Kiernan

A young boy shares his delight with his mother as he paddles in the water on Coney Island, New York.

Olympus OM 1N, 1.8/50 mm, Ilford 400/135, Exp. f16-1/250

### Viktor Kolar
CZECH REPUBLIC

Viktor Kolar has been a freelance photographer since 1984, and in 1991 he won the *Mother Jones* International Photography Award. Since 1994, he has been working as lecturer in documentary photography at FAMU Academy of Performing Arts in Ostrava, Czech Republic.

© 1992 Viktor Kolar

Spring song – Martie, aged six, entertains her one-year-old sister Terezie with a tune near Ostrava, Czech Republic.

Leica 111.B, 35 mm, NP7/135, Exp. f8-1/200

### Jerry Koontz
USA

Jerry Koontz has been a photographer for around 30 years. Jerry Koontz Photography specializes in photographing children, people and some landscapes, as well as weddings and portraits.

© 1997 Jerry Koontz

Liaza, aged 12, and her younger sister Adriana, six, captured as they play on the streets of Ajijic village in Mexico.

Nikon F5, Nikon 2.8/180 mm, Fuji Sensia/135, Exp. f4-1/125

### Dmitri Korobeinikov
RUSSIA

Dmitri Korobeinikov was born in Russia and became a photo-correspondent after graduating from the Kemerovo State Institute of Cultural Work. In 1975 and 1985, he was the Laureate International Photo Journalist for InterPress Photo. Currently Dmitri works for the Russian Information Agency, Novosti, based in Moscow.

© 1989 Dmitri Korobeinikov

In the Russian village of Gimenej, heavy rain turns the road to mud on a couple's wedding day. The bridegroom helps to push the car as his bride seeks sanctuary from the weather.

Nikon FE2, 35 mm, Cbema 200/135, Exp. f5.6-1/125

### Tamás Kovács
HUNGARY

Tamás Kovács has been a professional photographer since 1988. Currently he works for the Hungarian News Agency and is based in Budapest.

© 1999 Tamás Kovács

An emotional scene in Vàc, Hungary, as a Gypsy family mourns the tragic death of a young boy. Fourteen-year-old Krisztian was stabbed by classmates who claimed that he was a racketeer. Amid the sorrow, a traditional Gypsy band plays his favourite songs.

Nikon F3, 28 mm, Kodak/135, Exp. f5.6-1/60

### Herman Krieger
USA

Herman Krieger began his career working in the photo department of Packard Motor Company in the USA and freelancing for local newspapers. After taking a degree in mathematics at the University of California, Berkeley, he moved to Europe to work as a computer programmer. He resumed his interest in photography by taking a Bachelor of Fine Arts degree at the University of Oregon, publishing a book and exhibiting in various galleries. Herman is now an Associate of the Royal Photographic Society.

© 1994 Herman Krieger

Surrounded by pictures of her loved ones, 92-year-old Frances reminisces on family life at her home in Oregon, USA.

Fuji GW690II, 90 mm, Kodak T-max 400/120, Exp. N/A

### Philip Kuruvita
AUSTRALIA

Philip Kuruvita lives in Launceston, Tasmania, and works as a professional photographer. He was awarded the Master statue from the Australian Institute of Professional Photography in 1999 and was the Tasmanian Professional Photographer of the Year 2000.

© 1999 Philip Kuruvita

A woodshed in Tasmania, Australia, provides an unusual playground for identical twins, Summer and Melody.

Leica M6, 35 mm, Kodak T-max/135, Exp. N/A

### Slim Labidi
FRANCE

Slim Labidi (professional name: SLim SFax) has been an active photographer since 1989. Born in Tunis, he has lived in Lyons in France since the age of three.

© 1996 SLim SFax

One-month-old Malik is the centre of attention for his loving parents, Cecile and Hafid, photographed at their home in Villeurbaine, France.

Minolta 7xi, 28–105 mm, Ilford Delta Pro/135, Exp. f3.5-1/125

### Mark LaRocca
USA

Mark LaRocca's interest in photography began at an early age when his grandfather, a keen amateur photographer, showed him slides of his travels around the world. After obtaining degrees in engineering and Latin American history from Cornell University in New York, Mark studied at the International Center of Photography, also in New York. Currently he works as a freelance documentary photographer.

© 1998 Mark LaRocca

A mother's joyous smile as she admires her newborn baby, Cedric, born 36 hours ago at this hospital in Newton, Massachusetts, USA.

Rolleiflex 2.8F, 80 mm, Kodak Tri-X/120, Exp. f2.8-1/60

### Ben Law-Viljoen
USA

Ben Law-Viljoen is a chemistry and biochemistry graduate of Rhodes University, South Africa. He also studied photography in the Fine Art department of the university and now works as a freelance photographer and printer in the USA.

© 1996 Ben Law-Viljoen

Sixty years on – Fransiena, 84, holds a bunch of wild mustard flowers picked for her by Willem, 93. The couple are celebrating over six decades of marriage and stand outside the home they share in Haarlem, South Africa.

Pentax 6x7, 4/45 mm, Agfa Optima/120, Exp. f22-1/30

### Thanh Long
VIETNAM

Thanh Long developed his first film over 35 years ago and is still a professional photographer in Nha Trang city, Vietnam. He has won gold medals at the Asahi Shimbun International Photographic Salon of Japan in 1988, 1995, 1997 and 1999. His work has been exhibited through Europe, Asia and North America.

© 1995 Thanh Long

Innocence and wisdom captured on film in Phan Rang city, Vietnam. New life is nurtured by age-old experience as this 86-year-old grandmother shares a tender moment with her grandson.

Nikon F2, 2.8/28 mm, Kodak Tri-X 400/135, Exp. f8-1/30

### Georgina Lucock
AUSTRALIA

Georgina Lucock studied for a Bachelor of Visual Arts degree in Australia, majoring in photography. Since graduating in 1987, she has completed a wide range of photographic assignments, including work for magazines, architectural and design companies.

© 1999 Georgina Lucock

A quiet moment – parents Kevin and Annette tenderly embrace 10-month-old Jai during a family photo session in Bellingen, Australia.

Mamiya TLR, C330 80 mm, Ilford FP4 Plus/120, Exp. f2.8/5.5-1/250

### Richard Majchrzak
SOLOMON ISLANDS

Richard Majchrzak was born near Heidelberg, Germany, and studied anthropology and philosophy in Goettingen and Berlin. He worked for a publication where he was photographer, writer, reproduction photographer and layout artist. He is a long-time contributor to the *Gruene Kraft*, has travelled extensively and currently lives in Honiara, Solomon Islands.

© 1996 Richard Majchrzak

This family portrait shows the traditional tattoos of Ontong Java, Solomon Islands. Men and women tattooed their bodies for beauty and status, before the church discouraged this old custom.

Leica R3, 50 mm, Fujichrome/135, Exp. N/A

### Dave Marcheterre
CANADA

Dave Marcheterre is a graduate of the CEGEP de Matane in Quebec, Canada, and the University of Quebec. Currently he is based in Montreal where he works as a photographer and graphic designer.

© 1997 Dave Marcheterre

Cheek to cheek – father and daughter hold each other close on a chilly morning in Gaspésie, Quebec, Canada.

Contax 137 MA, 135 mm, Kodak/135, Exp. N/A

### Jenny Matthews
UK

Jenny Matthews has been a photographer since 1982, documenting social issues in Britain and abroad. She has worked extensively in Latin America and Africa, and has undertaken many commissions for development organizations such as Save The Children and Oxfam. Jenny was a founder member of Format, a women's photo agency.

© 1995 Jenny Matthews

An emotional embrace – in Rwanda, Africa, Epiphanie is reunited with her niece and only surviving relative, Uwimana. Her own children were victims of the country's genocide.

Nikon F4, 50 mm, Kodak Tri-X/135, Exp. f5.6-1/60

### Stephen McAlpine
AUSTRALIA

Stephen McAlpine graduated from Griffith University in Brisbane, Australia, and taught intellectually impaired children until he established his photography business in 1995. He is currently working towards his Master of Photography with the Australian Institute of Professional Photographers.

© 1996 Stephen McAlpine

A grandmother's gaze – as she joins her family in celebrating her granddaughter's wedding in Brisbane, Australia.

Nikon F4, 2.8/80–200 mm, Kodak TMY/135, Exp. f4-1/125

### Tony McDonough
AUSTRALIA

Tony McDonough was born in Liverpool, England, and emigrated to Australia in the 1960s. He has worked on newspapers and magazines for over 20 years, covering news, features and sport.

© 1996 Tony McDonough

Welcome to the world – a father captures on film the very first breath of his new daughter, Sophie. She was born by Caesarean section at a hospital in Attadale, Australia.

Nikon F90X, 35–70 mm, Fuji 800/135, Exp. f5.6-1/250

### Leigh Mitchell-Anyon
NEW ZEALAND

Leigh Mitchell-Anyon is a Master of Photography of the New Zealand Institute of Professional Photographers. He won the Champion Print section of their annual awards in 1991, and the Portrait section in 1996. Currently Leigh is working as a commercial and editorial photographer.

© 1988 Leigh Mitchell-Anyon

Family holiday – dressing down for summer on Waiheke Island in Auckland, New Zealand.

Leica M3, 3.5/35 mm, Kodak GA100/135, Exp. f8-1/125

### Stacey P Morgan
USA

Stacey P Morgan has been a professional photojournalist for over 15 years. She has been a contract photographer for the *New York Times*, the *Baltimore Sun* and the *Philadelphia Inquirer*. Her work has also appeared in magazines including *Sports Illustrated*, *Golf Illustrated* and *Vogue*. Stacey has won over 40 awards in national and international competitions, and has exhibited work in galleries, museums and collections around the world.

© 1992 Stacey P Morgan

Bathtime story in Chester Springs, Pennsylvania, USA. Five-year-old Devin listens intently to his grandfather reading.

Nikon F3, 2.8/20 mm, Kodak Tri-X/135, Exp. N/A

### Rashid Un Nabi
BANGLADESH

Rashid Un Nabi is Registrar at the Department of Radiotherapy at Chittagong Medical College Hospital, Bangladesh. Apart from being a cancer specialist, he has won 30 national and over 40 international awards for his photography since 1986. He also has an award of excellence from FIAP, the International Federation of Photographic Art.

© 1994 Rashid Un Nabi

These twin brothers were caught on film as they made their way down Elephant Road in Dhaka, Bangladesh. One brother, crippled since birth, is carried by his twin.

Contax 159 mm, Tamron SP 70–210 mm, Konica Super XG 100/135, Exp. N/A

### Toshihiro Ogasawara
JAPAN

Toshihiro Ogasawara was born in Hyogo, Japan. He graduated from the Japan Photograph Institute in 1997 and now works as a freelance photographer.

© 1999 Toshihiro Ogasawara

Bathtime becomes playtime for Atsuki and his young sons, Yuya, aged one, and Kazuki, three, at the family home in Hyogo, Japan.

Canon IOS 1, 28–105 mm, Fuji Monochrome 400/135, Exp. f5.6-1/60

### J Michael O'Grady
USA

J Michael O'Grady runs a communications technology business in Maryland, USA, and has been a keen amateur photographer since the age of 16.

© 1998 J Michael O'Grady

The photographer's daughter Maggie, aged three, is intrigued by the antics of her five-year-old brother Patrick in the family garden in Frederick, Maryland, USA.

Nikon FM2, 85 mm, Kodak T-max 100/135, Exp. N/A

### Adriaan Oosthuizen
SOUTH AFRICA

Adriaan Oosthuizen trained as a conservationist in South Africa. His serious interest in photography began when he travelled to London and worked as a photographer's assistant. He now works as a full-time photographer based in Cape Town, South Africa.

© 1993 Adriaan Oosthuizen

A quiet moment as a Chelsea Pensioner, in distinctive red and black uniform, enjoys the company of his daughter in a park in London, England. The Chelsea Pensioners are war veterans or retired military personnel.

Canon EOS 1, 28–70 mm, Kodak/135, Exp. f5.6-1/60

### Ray Peek
AUSTRALIA

Ray Peek began his photography career in 1947 and set up his own business in 1955, specializing in weddings, portrait and press photography. In 1989 he won the main prize in the Hasselblad Portrait Competition, and in 1999 second prize in the Hasselblad Old Masters Competition.

© 1991 Ray Peek

Another generation learns about mustering from the head of the family. "Big" Morrie Dingle, a grazier in South Queensland, Australia, and his two grandsons take a break from the saddle to enjoy some food.

Hasselblad 500 CM, 150 mm, Kodak T-max 400/120, Exp. f8-1/125

### Rachel Pfotenhauer
USA

Rachel Pfotenhauer is based in Colorado, USA, and has been taking photographs for eight years. She has concentrated on documentary and editorial work, as well as undertaking commercial and stock photography. Rachel is also a writer, and her words and images have appeared in several magazines, newspapers and books.

© 1999 Rachel Pfotenhauer

Circles of celebration – surrounded by their family, Jean and Paul celebrate their 50th wedding anniversary at Lake Tahoe, California, USA. Reunited for this special occasion, their children and grandchildren dance in circles around the delighted couple.

Nikon N90, 35–80 mm, Kodak/135, Exp. f4-1/15

### Heather Pillar
TAIWAN

Heather Pillar worked as a professional photographer in Boston, USA, for 10 years before moving to Taipei, Taiwan, to teach art. While in Boston, she spent six months documenting the moving story of Morrie Schwartz and his battle with amytrophic lateral sclerosis (ALS), also known as Lou Gehrig's disease.

© 1995 Heather Pillar

Rob Schwartz with his father Morrie. Mitch Albom, a writer and former student of Morrie, noticed Morrie on a television show and renewed contact with his old professor. The outcome was Albom's moving bestseller *Tuesdays with Morrie*, based on time spent with Morrie on the last 14 Tuesdays of his life.

Canon EOS A2, 50 mm, Kodak T-max 400/135, Exp. f4-1/30

### Linda Pottage
AUSTRALIA

Linda Pottage lives in Victoria, Australia. After beginning her career as a writer, she launched her own clothing label and worked as a stylist for photographers working on her fashion promotions. Her interest in photography blossomed and Linda is now a working photographer, specializing in portraits. She has won several awards and has appeared in photographic exhibitions in Melbourne.

© 1999 Linda Pottage

Bedecked with garlands of white daisies, a cherished family member is buried on a mid-winter morning in Menzies Creek, Victoria, Australia. The photographer, right, with her children, Zeke, Zoë and Jesse, say their last goodbyes as they lay Leo to rest beneath the plum tree.

Canon EOS 1N, 55 mm, Kodak T-max/135 Exp. N/A

### Duane Prentice
CANADA

Duane Prentice began his career in El Salvador in 1987. He has undertaken diverse photographic assignments around the world, including work with Médecins sans Frontières and the flying eye doctor service, Orbis International. Duane's work has appeared in various international publications including *Life* magazine.

© 1983 Duane Prentice

Generations apart but bound by family love – Dolma and her great-grandmother sit together in quiet contentment on the roof of their home in Ladakh, northern India.

Canon A1, 105 mm, Agfa Scala slide/135, Exp. f11-1/125

### Guus Rijven
THE NETHERLANDS

Guus Rijven studied architecture and graphic design in his native Netherlands, and now works as a freelance photographer and designer. His work has been displayed in New York, Jakarta, Tokyo and Vancouver, as well as in the Netherlands. Guus teaches at the Royal Academy of Fine Arts in The Hague.

© 1997 Guus Rijven

Overcoming the generation gap in Brummen, the Netherlands. Eighty-one years separate a grandfather from his only grandchild, but that's no barrier to play. Two-year-old Jarón chooses the game.

Contax 91, 28 mm, Kodak Tri-X, Exp. N/A

© 1995 Guus Rijven

Holiday in the countryside of La Romagne, France – freezing temperatures, hungry woodstoves and just enough hot water for the kitchen sink. Four-month-old Jarón is quite happy to be washed alongside the pots and pans.

Rolleiflex 3.5, 75 mm, Kodak Tri-X/120, Exp. N/A

### Gabi Reichert
GERMANY

Gabi Reichert is a full-time mother of three. She has been a keen amateur photographer for nearly 20 years.

© 1999 Gabi Reichert

Bubenheim, Germany – eight-month-old Amy Sophia is a picture of contentment as she shares bath time with her photographer mother, Gabi.

Contax AX, 85 mm, Fuji Neopan 1600/135, Exp. f2.8-1/60

### Martin Rosenthal
ARGENTINA

Martin Rosenthal studied photography at the School of the Museum of Fine Arts in Boston, USA. A full-time photographer since 1992, he is based in Argentina and has travelled across Latin America with his work.

© 1995 Martin Rosenthal

A father and his children in Juanchaco, Colombia.

Nikon F3 HP, 35 mm, Kodak T-max 400/135, Exp. f8-1/125

### Deborah Roundtree
USA

Deborah Roundtree is a past member of the faculty at the Art Center College of Design in Pasadena, California, and the Academy of Art College in San Francisco. She has been president of Advertising Photographers of America National and has undertaken photographic assignments for a wide range of advertising clients. Deborah's work is displayed in the Permanent Collection of the Library of Congress, as well as in several private collections.

© 1999 Deborah Roundtree

The surprise party – a grandmother delights in the company of her grandchildren as she celebrates her 85th birthday in Yakima, Washington, USA.

N/A

### Sefton Samuels
UK

Sefton Samuels was a qualified textile technologist who developed a passion for photography and became a Member of the Royal Photographic Society. As the textile trade declined, Sefton became a full-time freelance photographer. He has worked for the BBC, ITN and Granada, as well as building up his own photo library.

© 1978 Sefton Samuels

During a family photo session in Altrincham, Cheshire, England, one-year-old Philip looks unimpressed by the behaviour of his older sister, Alice.

Rolleicord VA, 75 mm, Ilford HP4/120, Exp. f5.6-1/60

### Neil Selkirk
USA

Neil Selkirk was born in England and moved to the USA. Here he studied with photographer Diane Arbus and, following her death, researched and printed her photographs for the landmark Museum of Modern Art retrospective of her work. His images have appeared in many major American magazines including *Esquire*, *Vogue*, *Vanity Fair* and the *New Yorker*. He has also been involved in first issues and covers for new publications such as *Wired* and *The Movies*.

© 1984 Neil Selkirk

Open wide – on a trip to the beach in Wellfleet, Massachusetts, USA, nothing interests Zane more than her mother, Susan.

Rolleiflex 2.8, 80 mm, Agfapan 100/120, Exp. N/A

### Russell Shakespeare
AUSTRALIA

Russell Shakespeare studied photography at the Queensland College of Art in Brisbane, Australia. Currently he is staff photographer at the *Australian Magazine*. In 1995, Russell won the Nikon Press Photo of the Year (News), and in 1996 the Walkley Award for Best News Picture. Both of these awards are for work within the Australian media.

© 1998 Russell Shakespeare

In Manly, New South Wales, Australia, five-month-old Camille has a captive audience in her mother, Toni, and visiting grandparents, Margaret and Handley.

Leica M6, 28 mm, Kodak T-max/135, Exp. f4-1/15

### Cheryl Shoji
CANADA

Cheryl Shoji was born in Toronto, Canada, and is a graduate of the city's York University. She began her professional career on the *Canadian Magazine* and has since worked for a variety of other publications. Currently Cheryl is Photo Assignment Editor for the *Vancouver Sun* in Canada.

© 1982 Cheryl Shoji

In Burnaby, British Columbia, Canada, proud grandmother Dorothy soothes her first grandson as he expresses displeasure at a not-so-dry diaper.

Canon AE1, Kodak/135, Exp. N/A

### Steven Siewert
AUSTRALIA

Steven Siewert is a photographer with the *Sydney Morning Herald* in Australia. He has covered stories in various parts of the world including Rwanda, Indonesia and Papua New Guinea. Steven has been a winner of the Leica Australian Documentary Award, the Australian Press Photographer Award, and the Picture of the Year Award.

© 1994 Steven Siewert

An Aboriginal brother and sister can't hold back the smiles as their photograph is taken in Queensland, Australia.

Nikon F90X, Macro 55 mm, Ilford XP2/135, Exp. f8-1/500

### Les Slesnick
USA

After receiving a degree in pharmacy in 1965, Les Slesnick went on to gain a Master of Fine Art in photography from the Savannah (Georgia) College of Art and Design in 1993. He has been an exhibiting fine art photographer since 1974, a teacher of colour printing at the Crealde School of Art in Florida, and more recently Adjunct Professor of Photography at the University of Central Florida.

© 1998 Les Slesnick

**WINNER OF THE "FAMILY" CATEGORY AND THE OVERALL GRAND PRIZE IN THE M.I.L.K. PHOTOGRAPHIC COMPETITION.**

© 1998 Les Slesnick

Personal portraits, Mexico – the essence of a household, its furnishings and cherished memorabilia, offer an insightful glimpse into the owner's life. Part of the "Private Spaces" collection, the series celebrates the small details and simple beauty found in every home.

Canon A1, 24 mm, Kodak/135, Exp. f8

## Christopher Smith
USA

Christopher Smith was born in Atlanta, Georgia, USA. He began his photographic career in 1986 taking pictures of whitewater rafters in Maine and went on to study with the Maine Photographic Workshop. He then moved to North Carolina where he has been a freelance photographer since 1991.

© 1998 Christopher Smith

Age is no barrier to enjoying a dance at a wedding party in North Carolina, USA. New bride, Pamela, teaches Uncle Mac the steps, while the bride's parents show how it should be done.

Nikon F5, 2.8/35–70 mm, Fuji NPH/135, Exp. f5.6-1/125

## Linda Sole
UK

Linda Sole is a freelance photographer based in South-East London. She specializes in reportage, and her work has been published in various magazines and books. Linda was the winner of the Channel 4 and *Evening Standard* "Big City" competition in 1993, and a category winner of the Image Bank Campaign 1997. She is a member of the Independent Photography Project.

© 1999 Linda Sole

When her daughter Judith became pregnant, English photographer Linda Sole decided to make this her next project. Judith is enjoying a bath on a hot summer day in Woolwich, London – two months later a daughter, Rose, was born.

Leica M6, 28 mm, Kodak Tri-X 400/135, Exp. f5.6-1/60

## Fredé Spencer
DENMARK

Fredé Spencer was born in Denmark and studied photography at Nottingham Trent University in England. He spent his final year focusing on underwater photography and is pursuing this speciality as his career.

© 1999 Fredé Spencer

Water baby – swimming under water comes perfectly naturally to baby Louis. He and his mother, Dimiti, enjoy a swimming class for "Little Dippers" in London, England.

Nikon 6006, 28 mm, Kodak GPX 160/135, Exp.f8-1/125

### Petra Stepan
CZECH REPUBLIC

Petra Stepan was born in Brno, Czech Republic. She graduated with a Master of Art (MA) from FAMU Academy of Performing Arts in Prague in 1999. She then won a scholarship to study at the Academy of Fine Arts in Milan. Petra has exhibited in the Czech Republic and elsewhere in Europe.

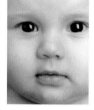

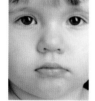

© 1998 Petra Stepan

Family resemblance – the Vancura family of Valasske Mezerici, Czech Republic. These photographs show the six children of parents Tatana and Hynek – Terezie, Jan, Barbora, Johana, Adela and Klara. Their first child was born in 1991 and their sixth child in 1997, and all were delivered by Caesarean section. These images portray the unique physiognomy of the family. Since this series was taken, the Vancuras have had a seventh child, Sara.

Asahi Pentax 6x7, Takumar 1:4/200 mm, Ilford Pan 100/120, Exp. f22

### Edmond Terakopian
UK

Edmond Terakopian has been a press photographer for over 10 years. Currently he works for the *Harrow Observer*, and does freelance work for the *Guardian* newspaper and *Time Out* magazine. He is a contributing photographer for the GAMMA agency in France, and Apeiron in Greece.

© 1991 Edmond Terakopian

A family is reunited. British Royal Air Force sergeant John has just returned from the Gulf War to his wife Sharon and their two-year-old son Phillip. Their reunion was captured during a press conference in Stanmore, Middlesex, England.

Canon F1N, 85 mm, Kodak/135, Exp. N/A

### Peter Thomann
GERMANY

Peter Thomann was born in Berlin and studied photography at the Folkwang School for Design. Since 1968 he has been a staff photographer for *Stern* magazine. He has won several awards including World Press Photo awards in 1963, 1964 and 1982. Peter was awarded the Kodak Photobook Award in 1993 for his book *Horses in Black and White Photographs*.

© 1975 Peter Thomann

When two-year-old Julian visits his grandparents' house in Emmendingen, Germany, he is fascinated by the smoke from grandfather Ernst's cigar.

Nikon F3, 35 mm, Kodak Tri-X/135, Exp. 1/30

### Chirasak Tolertmongkol ("G")
THAILAND

Chirasak Tolertmongkol is known simply as "G" among Thailand's professional photographers. He is a member of the Bangkok Photographic Society and has won many awards locally and internationally, including the "Honourable Citizen" from the Republic of China, and the Grand Prize in the "Thai Birds" competition.

© 1999 Chirasak Tolertmongkol

The sun sets over a hill tribe village in Chiang Rai, northern Thailand. While the parents gather in the middle of the village, their children use the main thoroughfare as their playground.

Canon EOS 1N, 20–70 mm, Fuji Velvia/135, Exp. f8-1/30

### Gordon Trice
USA

Gordon Trice's interest in photography began when he worked on a newspaper, followed by his experience as a corporate staff photographer in aviation. He has covered most areas of photography since his career began. Currently he works freelance for corporate and advertising clients, photographing people and products on location and in his studio.

© 1999 Gordon Trice

Father Heath holds his eight-month-old daughter, Bethany. This family portrait was photographed in Abilene, Texas, USA.

Fuji 680, 210 mm, Kodak/120, Exp. f16-1/250

### Luca Trovato
USA

Luca Trovato was born in Alessandria, Italy. After graduating from high school in Venezuela, he moved to California and studied photography in Santa Barbara. Luca is now a freelance photographer based in New York.

© 1998 Luca Trovato

The Gobi Desert, Mongolia – stranded with all their belongings, a nomadic family are relaxed as they await help.

Pentax 6x7, 2.8/90 mm, Fuji 160 NPS/120, Exp. f5.6-1/60 sec

### Natassa Tselepoglou
GREECE

Natassa Tselepoglou was born in Greece. After working in Italy as a fashion designer, she returned to her home country and began attending photography workshops. Today she works as a freelancer and has displayed her work in three solo exhibitions.

© 1999 Natassa Tselepoglou

Family life in Halkidiki, Greece. Three-year-old Lia and her mother, Daphne, put their feet up and share a fairy tale.

Canon F1, 3.5/35–105 ED, Kodak T-max 400/135, Exp. f11-1/125

### Lambro (Tsiliyiannis)
SOUTH AFRICA

Lambro is a South African freelance photographer. His work on travelogues, fashion and advertising campaigns has taken him to over 27 different countries.

© 1999 Lambro (Tsiliyiannis)

Two-year-old Robert greets his 85-year-old grandfather, Christy, in Cape Town, South Africa.

Canon EOS 3, 17–35 mm, Kodak T400 CN/135, Exp. f2.8/4-1/60

### Dô˜ Anh Tuâń
VIETNAM

Dô˜ Anh Tuâń has been a photographer since 1991 and is also an active musician and painter. He is a member of the Hanoi Artistic Photography Association and the Vietnamese Artistic Photography Association.

© 1997 Dô˜ Anh Tuâń

Grandmother and grandchildren – an affectionate family gathering outside their stilt house in the high plateaus of Quang Nam, Vietnam.

Nikon F3HP, 2.8/100 mm, Ilford HP5/135, Exp. f8-1/30

### Quoc Tuan
VIETNAM

Quoc Tuan was born in Saigon and has been a photographer for 20 years. During this time he has won several international prizes, including the Grand Prize Accu in Japan in 1999 and the second prize in Earth Vision Japan in 2000.

© 1999 Quoc Tuan

A grandfather and grandmother, both over the age of 70, are enchanted with their one-month-old grandson. They are playing with him on the verandah of their home in Ho Chi Minh City, Vietnam. The child was born on the couple's 50th wedding anniversary.

Nikon F70, 2.8/180 mm ED, Kodak T-max 400/135, Exp. f4-1/60

### Shaun Van Steyn
USA

Shaun Van Steyn was born in England and studied photography at the Corcoran School of Art in Washington, USA. His work has appeared in the *Washington Post*, *People*, *American Heritage* and *Time* magazines.

© 1980 Shaun Van Steyn

Last steps towards motherhood captured in Fairfax, Virginia, USA. Mother-to-be Carol is a day away from giving birth, while two-year-old Simon looks forward to the new addition to the family.

Nikon Nimormat, 50 mm, Kodak/135, Exp. f5.6-1/125

### Auke Vleer
THE NETHERLANDS

Auke Vleer graduated from St Joost Academy for Visual Arts in Breda, Netherlands, in 1992. He worked in New York for four years for clients including the *New York Times* magazine, *Marie Claire* and Island Records. Auke returned to Amsterdam in 1998.

© 1997 Auke Vleer

Five-year-old Pol with his aunt, Letty, on a family vacation in Baratier, France. While grandmother Fanny admires the view of the lake, their dog prefers to take a nap.

Graflex Crown graphic 4 x 5, 135 mm, Kodak Plus-X/4"x5", Exp. f11-1/30

© 1997 Auke Vleer

Young cousins – Pol, Joris, Dorus and Rik – enjoy being taken for a ride on the beach in Baratier, France.

Graflex Crown graphic 4 x 5, 135 mm, Kodak Plus-X/4"x5", Exp. f11-1/30

### Tong Wang
CHINA

Tong Wang was born in Jilin province in China and now lives in Ping Ding Shan City, Henan province. He took up photography in 1989, and from 1992 onwards has been photographing specialized subjects. His photographs have appeared in magazines including *Dili Zhishi (Geographic Knowledge)* and *Henan Huabao (Human Pictorial)*.

© 1998 Tong Wang

A father holds his sleeping child as he cycles through Zhengzhou, China.

Nikon F601, 28 mm, Kodak T-max 400/135, Exp.

### David Williams
UK

David Williams is a professional exhibiting photographer of a wide range of subject matter, from documentary to video art. Winner of the BBC Scotland 150 Years of Photography award, he is currently Head of Photography at Edinburgh College of Art.

© 1997 David Williams

Face to face – in Newcastle, England, godfather David meets his one-month-old godson, Samuel, for the first time.

Nikon FE, 55 mm, Kodak/135, Exp. f8

### Greg Williams
UK

Greg Williams is a reportage photographer based in London, England. His work appears regularly in *Le Figaro*, *Time*, *Stern* and the *Sunday Times* magazine. Greg is the director of the creative talent agency Growbag.

© 1998 Greg Williams

Brother and sister in Peterborough, England. Jason, aged nine, helps four-year-old Georgina to put on her prosthetic legs before they go out to play. Georgina is a second generation thalidomide victim.

Leica M6, 35 mm, Fuji 800/135, Exp. f4-1/60

### Manfred Wirtz
THE NETHERLANDS

Manfred Wirtz was born in Germany and today lives in Monnickendam, the Netherlands. He specializes in reportage and documentary photography. Manfred's work has appeared in exhibitions in the Netherlands, Germany, Belgium, Luxembourg and France. He has received honourable mentions from the Fujifilm European Press Award and the Photographers Association of the Netherlands.

© 1998 Manfred Wirtz

In a remote area of Romania, a new bride is dressed by her mother and three sisters. The ceremony symbolizes that she is leaving home to start a new life with her husband.

Contax AX, 35–135 mm, Fuji Superia 800/135, Exp. N/A

### Jim Witmer
USA

Jim Witmer has been a professional photographer for 18 years and currently works as a photojournalist for the *Dayton Daily News* in Ohio, USA. His work has been published worldwide in magazines such as *Life*, *Time* and *Sports Illustrated*.

© 1996 Jim Witmer

A photographer father takes a self-portrait with his one-year-old son, Adam, at home in Troy, Ohio, USA.

Nikon F4, 80–200 mm, Kodak/135, Exp. f8-1/250

© 1998 Jim Witmer

A family prays in a hospital room in Cleveland, Ohio, USA. Dwayne, far right, is moments away from undergoing surgery to remove one of his kidneys. It will be transplanted into his cousin Calvin, second from left, who is suffering from kidney disease.

Nikon F4, 80–200 mm, Fuji 800/135, Exp. f2.8-1/125

### Guan Cheong Wong
MALAYSIA

Guan Cheong Wong has been a member of the Penang Photography Society in Malaysia since 1981. He has taken part in many local and international competitions, and has acted as judge for the Penang International Photo Salon.

© 1996 Guan Cheong Wong

Front and back – in the Cameron Highlands, Malaysia, a mother carries her children in the traditional way of the Orang Asli people.

Nikon F801, 1.8/85 mm, Fuji/135, Exp. f8-1/60

### Jia Lin Wu
CHINA

Jia Lin Wu was born in Yunnan province, China. He graduated from the Affiliated Middle School of Yunnan University in 1961 and began working in photography eight years later. Since then, his work has appeared in several exhibitions and books. In 1997 he received the *Mother Jones* Documentary Photographic Award.

© 1989 Jia Lin Wu

Mother and son captured on film in Butuo County, Sichuan province, China.

Nikon, 35–70 mm, Kodak T-max/135, Exp. N/A

## M·I·L·K

MOMENTS   INTIMACY   LAUGHTER   KINSHIP

First published in Australia in 2002 by Hodder Headline Australia Pty Limited [a member of the Hodder Headline Group], Level 22, 201 Kent Street, Sydney NSW 2000.

First published in New Zealand in 2002 by Hodder Moa Beckett Publishers [a member of the Hodder Headline Group], 4 Whetu Place, Mairangi Bay, Auckland, New Zealand.

The following individuals, companies, and organizations were significant contributors to the development of M.I.L.K. – Ruth Hamilton, Ruth-Anna Hobday, Claudia Hood, Nicola Henderson, Liz McRae, Brian Ross, Don Neely, Kai Brethouwer, Vicki Smith, Rebecca Swan, Bound to Last, Designworks, Image Centre Limited, Logan Brewer Production Design Limited, KPMG Legal, Lowe Lintas & Partners, Midas Printing Group Limited, MTA Arts for Transit, Print Management Consultants, Sauvage Design, Mary-Ann Lewis, Vibeke Brethouwer and Karen Pearson.

Special thanks also to David Baldock, Julika Batten, Anne Bayin, Sue Bidwill, Janet Blackwell, John Blackwell, Susanna Blackwell, Sandra Bloodworth, Sonia Carroll, Mona Chen, Patrick Cox, Malcolm Edwards, Michael Fleck, Lisa Highton, Anne Hoy, C K Lau, Liz Meyers, James Mora, Paddianne Neely, Grant Nola, Ricardo Ordóñez, Kim Phuc, Chris Pitt, Tanya Robertson, Margaret Sinclair, Marlis Teubner, Nicki White.

The publisher is grateful for permission to reproduce those items below subject to copyright. While every effort has been made to trace copyright holders, the publisher would be pleased to hear from any not acknowledged here.

Judith Wright extract from "Woman to Child" in *A Human Pattern: Selected Poems* (ETT Imprint, Sydney 1996); Morrie Schwatrz extract from *Morrie: In His Own Words*, reprinted by permission of Walker & Company.

Competition Chief Judge Elliott Erwitt. Designed by Lucy Richardson. Printed by Midas Printing Limited, Hong Kong.

ISBN 0 7336 1558 9